Writings of Julian of Norwich

Upper Room Spiritual Classics®

Selected, edited, and introduced by
KEITH BEASLEY-TOPLIFFE

UPPER
ROOM BOOKS®
NASHVILLE

WRITINGS OF JULIAN OF NORWICH

Copyright © 1998 by Upper Room Books

Previously published as *Encounter with God's Love: Selected Writings of Julian of Norwich*

All rights reserved.

Upper Room Books˙ website: books.upperroom.org

Upper Room˙, Upper Room Books˙, and design logos are trademarks owned by The Upper Room˙, Nashville, Tennessee. All rights reserved.

Scripture quotations are from the New Revised Standard Version Bible, copyright 1989 National Council of the Churches of Christ in the United States of America. Used by permission. All rights reserved.

Selections taken from *A Book of Showings to the Anchoress Julian of Norwich*, edited by Edmund College, OSA and James Walsh, SJ, Studies and Texts 35 (Toronto: Pontifical Institute of Mediaeval Studies, 1978). Used by permission.

Cover design: Tim Green | Faceout Studio

Interior design and typesetting: PerfecType, Nashville, TN

ISBN 978-0-8358-1651-9 (print) | ISBN 978-0-8358-1685-4 (mobi) | ISBN 978-0-8358-1686-1 (epub)

Library of Congress Cataloging-in-Publication Data

Julian of Norwich, b. 1343.

[Revelations of divine love. English. Selections]

Encounter with God's love: selected writings of Julian of Norwich.

p. cm.—(Upper Room spiritual classics. Series 2)

ISBN 0-8358-0833-5

1. Love—Religious aspects—Christianity—Prayer-books and devotions—English. 2. Devotional literature, English (Middle). 3. Julian of Norwich, b. 1343. 4. Title. II. Series.

BV4832.2.J8513 1998

242—dc21   97-30641

CIP

Contents

Introduction

Many Christian spiritual classics offer advice on how to pray and live a Christian life. In the writings of a late-fourteenth-century Englishwoman known as Julian of Norwich we have something different. Julian offers us a report on what she has learned about God through a lifetime of prayer.

When she was thirty, Julian received a series of visions or revelations in the midst of a severe illness. For the next twenty years she continued to meditate on the meaning of these visions. The result is one of the most profound discussions of God's love working through mercy and grace in all of Christian literature. She shares her experience of a God determined to protect us "most securely" from the dangers of sin and to raise us up whenever we fall, whose love fulfills and surpasses the ideals of both fatherly and motherly love.

Julian's World

The fourteenth century was one of the most troubled times in all of European history. The Hundred Years War between

England and France began in 1337 and smoldered for another 116 years. England was also torn by war with Scotland, internal struggles between the king and barons, and one major peasant revolt. Far more devastating than any war, the Black Death (bubonic plague) came to England in 1348. Although census records are poor, anywhere from a third to a half of the population died in two years. Outbreaks continued throughout the century, with a major one in 1361.

One response to the overwhelming presence of death was a renewed interest in the spirit. There was a flowering of writings on the spiritual life. Richard Rolle (1300–49), the unknown author of *The Cloud of Unknowing*, Walter Hilton (d. 1396), and Julian herself created a distinctively English approach to the spiritual life, strongly influenced by the writings of "Dionysius the Areopagite" (now known to be a fifth-century Syrian monk, but then thought to be a convert of Saint Paul), first translated into English by the author of *The Cloud of Unknowing*. At the same time, calls for reform of the church were beginning with Oxford professor John Wycliffe (c. 1330–84). Julian herself shows great interest in "Holy Church" as the body of Christ, but little in the earthly workings or hierarchy of the church.

In addition to the technical language of spiritual theology, Julian is also fond of the language of knightly romance. In particular, the words *courteous* and *courtesy* are among her favorite terms for Christ's action. Here *courteous* does not mean simply "polite" but describes the ideal of all that a knight should be: brave, good, gentle with those who are weak, merciful toward his enemies, devoted to those he loves, noble in action as he is noble by birth.

Julian's Life

Very little is known of Julian's life apart from what she reveals. She says that her revelations took place on May 13, 1373, when she was thirty and a half years old. That would place her birth near the end of 1342, six years before the Black Death came to England. She apparently wrote a brief account shortly after recovering from her illness. About twenty years later she wrote a greatly expanded version (nearly three times the length). She explains that she still had not fully understood the revelations for "twenty years less three months." A preface to a copy of the short version describes her as "a devout woman and her name is Julian, who is a recluse at Norwich and still alive, anno domini 1413." She is also mentioned in a few wills (the last from 1416) and in the writing of Margery Kempe, a sort of "spiritual tourist" who visited Julian about 1413.

Although Julian claims to be "a simple, unlettered creature," this is surely a conventional disclaimer. As a woman she could not claim to be a theologian, but she might be allowed to write about her own experiences. Her writing, though, shows evidence of extensive study and considerable literary skill. She knew the works of Rolle, Hilton, and the author of *The Cloud of Unknowing*, as well as Chaucer's translation of Boethius and various other works. She was thoroughly acquainted with the Bible (especially John's Gospel and Paul's letters), though she rarely quotes it directly.

This education must have come through a long time spent as a nun, since only a convent could provide it. She was probably still in the convent (some have suggested the Benedictine convent near Norwich) when she had her revelations, and perhaps long after. Eventually she became an anchoress at the church of Saint Julian in Norwich, which was then the second largest city of England, after London. (The church was named for an earlier [male] saint, and Julian may have taken her name from the church.) As an anchoress, she lived alone (or perhaps with a maid) in a cell built onto the church. She probably followed the guidelines for such a life laid down in the *Ancrene Riwle* (Guide for Anchoresses), written about 1200. She might have made use of the extensive library in the Augustinian friary across the street from Saint Julian's church. When she moved there is unknown, but she was certainly there from before 1394 until her death sometime after 1415.

The church of Saint Julian and the cell where Julian of Norwich lived have been restored and rebuilt several times, most recently following bombing in 1942.

Further Reading

The modern critical edition of Julian is *A Book of Showings to the Anchoress Julian of Norwich* edited by Edmund Colledge, O.S.A. and James Walsh, S.J. (Toronto: Pontifical Institute of Mediaeval Studies, 1978). It contains the full text of both the long and short versions in Middle English, along with an excellent introduction and thorough notes concerning language, references to scripture and other writings, and literary devices. Colledge and Walsh also produced a modern translation of both versions published by Paulist Press.

The writings of Richard Rolle, Walter Hilton, and the author of *The Cloud of Unknowing* are available in many modern translations, including ones published by Paulist Press. The writings of Dionysius the Areopagite (or Pseudo-Dionysius) are also available in English.

A Distant Mirror: The Calamitous 14th Century by Barbara Tuchman is a fascinating introduction to the period, though Julian and the other English mystics are not mentioned.

Note on the Text

These selections represent a new and contemporary translation from the late-fourteenth-century English in Colledge and Walsh's critical edition of the long version. They have been edited for length and for inclusive language. In some instances,

Julian's favorite words have been retained, even when modern usage might suggest other translations. These include *courtesy* (as described above), *almighty* (Julian contrasts *almighty* God with *unmighty* human beings), and *beholding* (often used as a technical term for contemplative prayer).

Julian's Illness

From Chapters 2–3, First Revelation

In this introductory passage, Julian describes her desire for true contrition (sorrow for her sins), compassion, and longing for God. She asked God for a sickness that would teach her the pain and fear of death and call to mind Christ's own suffering and death. It came when she was thirty years old.

This revelation was made to a simple, unlettered creature living in mortal flesh in the year of our Lord 1373, the thirteenth day of May. This creature had previously desired three gifts from God. The first was remembrance of the passion. The second was bodily sickness. The third was to have three wounds as God's gifts. For the first, I thought I had some feeling concerning the passion of Christ, but I desired to have more by the grace of God. I thought I would like to have lived at that time with Magdalene and with others who were Christ's lovers, so that I might have seen in person the passion that our Lord suffered for me, so that I might have suffered with him, as did others who loved him. And so I desired a bodily sight, in which I might have more knowledge of the bodily pains of our Savior and of the compassion of our Lady and of all his true lovers who were living at that time and saw his pains. For I wanted to be one of them and suffer with them. I never desired any other sight or vision of God until the soul left the body, for I believed I was saved by the mercy of God. This was my meaning, that because of that vision I would afterward have a truer remembrance of the passion of Christ. For the second, an earnest desire to have a bodily sickness as God's gift came to my mind with contrition, freely, without any seeking. I wanted that sickness to be severe enough to kill, so that I might in that sickness have received all the rites of the Holy Church, believing that I would die and that everyone who saw me might suppose the same. For within that sickness I wanted no manner of comfort from fleshly or earthly life. I desired to have all manner of pains, bodily and spiritual, that I should have if I were to die: all the fears and temptations of demons and all manner of other pains except for the actual departure of the soul. By this I meant to be purged by the mercy of God and then live more for the honor of God because of that sickness. I hoped that it might have been to my benefit when I died. For I desired to be soon with my God and Maker.

These two desires of the passion and of the sickness that I desired from God were with a condition, for I knew this was not the common way of prayer. Therefore I said, "Lord, you know what I want and, if it is your will, that I might have it. And if it is not your will, good Lord, do not be displeased, for

I will only as you will." In my youth I desired to have this sickness when I became thirty years old.

For the third, by the grace of God and teaching of Holy Church I conceived a mighty desire to receive three wounds in my life: the wound of true contrition, the wound of kind compassion, and the wound of longing for God with all my will. Just as I asked the other two with a condition, so I asked this third strongly without any condition. Those two desires passed from my mind and the third dwelled there continually.

And when I was thirty and a half years old, God sent me a bodily sickness in which I lay three days and nights. On the fourth night I took all the rites of Holy Church and expected I would not live till day. After this I lay two days and two nights. On the third night, I often expected I would pass away. So did those who were with me. And yet I felt a great reluctance to die, though not because of anything in earth that I wanted to live for nor for any pain that I was afraid of, for I trusted in God's mercy. But it was because I wanted to live to love God better and for a longer time, that I might by the grace of that living be able to know and love God better in the bliss of heaven. I thought all the time I had lived here so short a time in comparison to that endless bliss. I thought, *Good Lord, is my living no longer for your worship?* I understood in my reason and by the feeling of my pains that I should die. And I agreed fully with all the will of my heart to be at God's will.

Thus I endured until day. By then I felt my body was dead from the middle downward. My priest was sent for to be at my death. Before he came, I had turned up my eyes and could not speak. He set the cross before my face and said, "I have brought the image of your Savior. Look on it and comfort yourself with it." I thought I was well, for my eyes were turned up to heaven where I trust to come by the mercy of God. Nevertheless, I agreed to turn my eyes to the face of the crucifix, if I could, and so I did. I thought I might be able to look longer straight ahead than straight up. After this my sight began to fail. It became as dark around me in the room as if it had been night, except in the image of the cross, which remained in ordinary light, I do not know how. Everything besides the cross was ugly and fearful to me as if it were filled with demons.

After this the upper part of my body began to die so that I scarcely had any feeling. My greatest pain was shortness of breath and failing of life. Then I truly expected to have passed away. Then suddenly all my pain was taken from me, and I was as whole in the upper part of my body as I ever was before. I marveled at this sudden change. I thought it was a secret working of God and not natural. Yet I had no greater trust that I would live from this feeling of ease, nor was it a full sense of ease to me. I thought I would rather have been delivered from this world, for my heart was resigned to this with all its will.

Then came suddenly to my mind that I should desire the second wound of our Lord's gift and grace, that my body might be filled with awareness and feeling of his blessed passion, as I had prayed before. For I wanted his pains for my pains, with compassion and then longing for God. Thus I thought I might, with God's grace, have the wounds that I had desired before. But in this I desired no bodily sight or any kind of vision of God, but compassion as I thought a kind soul might have for our Lord Jesus, who for love became a mortal man. I desired to suffer with him, living in my mortal body as God would give me grace.

God's Love for All Creation

From Chapters 5–6, First Revelation

As Julian lay in bed and looked at the crucifix her priest had set before her, she saw the head begin to bleed from the crown of thorns. This was the first of her sixteen revelations.

At the same time that I saw this vision of the head bleeding, our good Lord showed a spiritual vision of his humble loving. I saw that he is to us everything that is good and helpful. He is our clothing that for love wraps us and winds about us and encloses us for tender love, that he may never leave us. And so in this vision I saw that he is everything good, as I understood it.

And then he showed a little thing, the size of a hazelnut, lying in the palm of my hand, as it seemed to me. It was as round as a ball. I looked at it with the eye of my understanding and thought, *What can this be?* It was answered generally thus: "It is all that is made." I marveled that it could last, for it was so little that it could suddenly have become nothing. I was answered in my understanding, "It lasts and ever shall, for God loves it." And so everything has being by the love of God.

In this little thing I saw three properties. The first is that God made it, the second that God loves it, and the third that God keeps it. But what did I behold there? Truly, the Maker, the Keeper, the Lover. For until I am substantially united to God, I may never have full rest nor true bliss. That is to say that I am so fastened to God that there is nothing that is made between my God and me.

This little thing that is made, I thought it might have fallen into nothingness. We need to know this, that we should delight in nothing that is made in order to love and have God who is unmade. This is why we are not all in ease of heart and soul, for we seek here rest in this thing that is so little where there is no rest and we do not know our God, who is almighty, all-wise, and all-good, who is true rest. God wants to be known, and it delights God that we rest in God. For nothing less than God is sufficient for us. This is why no soul is at rest until it is emptied of all things that are made. When it is willingly emptied for love, to have God that is all, then it is able to receive spiritual rest.

And also our good Lord showed that it is God's great pleasure that a soul come to God naked, plainly, and humbly. For this is the natural yearning of the soul by the touching of the Holy Spirit, as I understand from this revelation. God, of your goodness, grant me your self, for you are enough for me, and nothing less that I might ask would be worthy of you. And if

I ask for anything less, I still want more. But only in you do I have all.

This revelation was given to my understanding to teach our souls wisely to cling to the goodness of God. And at that same time our way of praying was brought to my mind, how out of ignorance of love we use many intermediaries. Then I saw truly that it is more worthy and delightful to God that we faithfully pray to God directly in divine goodness and cling there by divine grace with true understanding and steadfast belief. For the highest prayer is to the goodness of God, which comes down to us in the lowest degree of our need. It gave life to the soul and makes it live and grow in grace and virtue. It is nearest in nature and readiest in grace, for it is the same grace the soul seeks and always will seek until we know our God truly, who has enclosed us all in God's self.

We go upright, and the food in our bodies is closed up as in a well-made purse. When it becomes necessary, the purse opens and then closes again just as it should. God does not despise anything God made or disdain to serve us in the simplest of natural bodily functions, for love of the soul made in God's own likeness. For as the body is clothed in cloth and the flesh in skin and the bones in flesh and the heart in the torso, so are we, soul and body, clothed and enclosed in the goodness of God. Indeed, more truly, for they all vanish and waste away. The goodness of God is always whole and nearer to us, without any comparison. For truly our Lover desires that the soul cling to God with all its might, and that we be always clinging to God's goodness. For of all things that the heart may think, this pleases God most and is most quickly beneficial. For the soul is so preciously loved by the One who is highest that it is beyond the knowledge of all creatures.

That is to say, there is no creature made that can understand how much and how sweetly and how tenderly our Maker loves us. And so we may with God's grace and help stand in spiritual beholding with everlasting marveling at this high, surpassing, immeasurable love that our good Lord has for us. And therefore we may ask of our Lover with reverence all that we will, for our natural will is to have God, and God's good will is to have us, and we can never cease willing or loving until we have God in the fullness of joy. And then we can will no more, for God wants us to be occupied in knowing and loving until the time comes that we shall be fulfilled in heaven.

Bliss in Heaven and Delight on Earth

From Chapters 14–15, Sixth and Seventh Revelations

In the second through fifth revelations, Julian continues to see aspects of the crucifixion: the scourging of Christ and the discoloration of his face. She also sees how God's love is present in all things and how Satan is defeated in Christ's passion. In the next two revelations, her attention turns to blessings in heaven and experiences of well-being and sorrow on earth.

After this our Lord said, "I thank you for your service and the work of your youth." And in this my understanding was lifted up into heaven, where I saw our Lord God as a lord in his own house, one who has invited all his beloved friends to a solemn feast. Then I saw the lord taking no seat in his own house. But I saw him royally reign in his house, filling it all full of joy and mirth, endlessly gladdening and comforting his beloved friends most humbly and most courteously with marvelous melody in endless love and his own beautiful, blessed cheer. This glorious cheer of the Godhead fills all heaven with joy and bliss.

God showed three degrees of bliss that all souls who have served God in any degree on earth shall have in heaven. The first is the honor and thanks they shall receive from our Lord God when they are released from pain. This thanks is so high and so honorable that they will think it fills them, even if there were nothing else. For I thought that all the pain and effort suffered by all living people would not deserve the honor and thanks that each one who has willingly served God will have.

The second is that all the blessed creatures in heaven will see this honorable thanksgiving. God makes their service known to all in heaven. At this time, this example was shown. If a king thanks his subjects, it is a great honor to them. And if he makes it known to all the realm, then their honor is much increased.

The third is that, as new and desirable as it is at that time, so will it last without end. For I saw that whenever men or women truly turn to God, even for one day's service and the endless will to do more, they will have all these three degrees of bliss. And the more loving souls see this courtesy of God, the more willing they are to serve God all their lives.

And after this God showed a supreme spiritual delight in my soul. In this delight I was filled with everlasting sureness, strongly fastened without any painful fear. This feeling was so happy and so spiritual that I was all in peace, ease, and rest. There was nothing on earth that would have grieved me.

This lasted just a little while. Then I was left to myself in heaviness and weariness of my life and disgust with myself, so that I scarcely had the patience to live. There was no comfort or ease in this feeling. I still had faith, hope, and charity in truth, but very little feeling of them. Soon after this, our blessed Lord gave me again comfort and rest in my soul, delight and sureness so blissful and strong that no fear or sorrow or physical or spiritual pain that might be suffered could have made me uneasy. And then the pain came again to my feelings, and then the joy and delight, now the one and now the other, at various times, I suppose about twenty times. And in the time of joy I might have said with Saint Paul, "Nothing will separate me from the love of Christ." And in the pain I might have said with Saint Peter, "Lord, save me; I perish."

This vision was revealed to teach me that it is useful to some souls to feel this way, sometimes to be in comfort and sometimes to fail and be left to themselves. God wants us to know that God holds us with the same certainty whether we are in sorrow or well-being. For the profit of our souls we are sometimes left to ourselves, although our sin is not ever the cause. For during this time I did not sin so as to be left to myself. It was too sudden! Nor did I deserve the feeling of bliss. Our Lord gives it freely when God wills and allows us to be sorrowful sometimes, and both are one love. For it is God's will that we cling to God's comfort with all our might. For bliss is lasting, without end, and pain is passing and shall be brought to nothing for those who will be saved. Therefore it is not God's will that we follow the feeling of pain with sorrow and mourning, but we will suddenly pass over and remain in the endless delight that is God.

Jesus Our Heaven

From Chapters 17–18, Eighth Revelation

In the eighth revelation, Julian sees Christ's body begin to die and shrivel as the body loses all its moisture. She describes vividly how the flesh hangs in tatters and the body turns brown with clotted blood.

I saw four manners of drying. The first was loss of blood. The second was the pain following after. The third was that he was hanging up in the air as people hang a cloth to dry. The fourth was that the bodily nature demanded liquid and there was no comfort ministered to him. Ah, that pain was hard and grievous, but much more hard and grievous when the moisture failed and all began to dry and shrivel. These were two pains that showed in the blessed head. The first pertained to the drying while it was moist. The other came with the shriveling and drying, with the blowing of the wind outside that dried him still further and pained him with cold more than my heart can think. And for all the other pains that I saw, all I can say is too little, for it may not be told.

The showing of Christ's pains filled me full of pain. I knew well that he suffered only once, but he wanted to show it to me and fill me with remembrance, as I had desired before. And in all this time of Christ's presence, I felt no pain but his pains. Then I thought I had hardly known at all what pain it was I had asked for. Like a wretch I turned back, thinking that if I had known what it would be, I would not have dared to pray for it. For I thought my pains passed any bodily death. I thought, *Is any pain in hell like this?* And I was answered in my reason, "Hell is another pain, for there is despair. But of all pains that lead to salvation, this is the greatest: to see the lover suffer." How could any pain be greater than to see him suffer who is all my life, all my bliss, all my joy? Here I felt steadfastly that I loved Christ so much more than myself that there was no pain that could be suffered like the sorrow I had to see him in pain.

At this time I wanted to look away from the cross, but I dared not, for I knew well that while I beheld the cross I was safe and secure. Therefore I would not agree to put my soul in danger, for besides the cross there was no security from fear of demons.

Then a thought occurred to me, as if it had been said by a friend: *Look up to heaven to his Father.* And then I saw well with the faith that I felt that there was nothing between the cross and heaven that could harm me. I needed either to look up or to answer. So I answered inwardly with all the strength of my soul, *No, I may not, for you are my heaven.* I said this because I did not want to look up. For I would rather have been in that pain until doomsday than have come to heaven by any way but him.

So I was taught to choose Jesus for my heaven, though I only saw him in pain at that time. I desired no other heaven than Jesus, who will be my bliss when I come there. And this has always been a comfort to me, that I chose Jesus to be my heaven by his grace in all this time of passion and sorrow. And that was a lesson for me that I should always do so, to choose Jesus only as my heaven in well-being and in sorrow.

And though I had turned back like a wretch, saying that if I had known what the pain was I would have been unwilling to pray for it, now I saw truly that this was unwillingness and the domination of the flesh without the soul's agreement, for which God assigns no blame. For turning back and making a willful choice are two contraries, both of which I felt at this time. They are of two parts, the one outward, the other inward. The outward part is our mortal flesh, which is now in pain and now in sorrow and shall be in this life and which I felt strongly at this time. That was the part that turned back. The inward part is a high and blessed life, which is all in peace and love. This is more privately felt. And this is the part in which I strongly, wisely, and willfully chose Jesus as my heaven.

And in this I saw truly that the inward part is master and sovereign to the outward, not paying any attention to its will.

Instead, all its intent and will is set endlessly on being united to our Lord Jesus. The inward part draws the outward part by grace, and both will be united in bliss without end by the virtue of Christ.

Joy in Christ's Passion

From Chapters 22–23, Ninth Revelation

In the ninth revelation, Julian sees Christ's death on the cross, followed immediately by the assurance of his joy that his mission of salvation has been accomplished.

Then our good Lord asked, "Are you well pleased that I suffered for you?" I said, "Yes, thank you, good Lord. Yes, good Lord, and may you be blessed." Then Jesus our good Lord said, "If you are pleased, then I am pleased. It is a joy, a bliss, an endless delight to me that I suffered the passion for you. And if I could suffer more, I would suffer more." Following this, my understanding was lifted up into heaven, and there I saw three heavens. I marveled greatly at this sight, and thought, *I see three heavens, and all through the blessed humanity of Christ. None is more, none is less, none is higher, none is lower, but all are the same in bliss.*

For the first heaven, Christ showed me his Father, not in bodily likeness, but in property and working. That is to say, I saw in Christ what the Father is. The work of the Father is this: giving a reward to the Son, Jesus Christ. This gift and reward is so blissful to Jesus that his Father could have given him no reward that would have delighted him more. For the first heaven, that is the pleasing of the Father, appeared to me as a heaven that was fully blissful. For God is well pleased with all the deeds that Jesus did for our salvation, so that we are his not only through his purchase, but also by the courteous gift of his Father. We are his bliss, we his reward, we his honor, we his crown. And this was a singular marvel and fully delightful vision: that we are his crown.

This that I say is such great bliss to Jesus that he counts as nothing his work and his passion and his cruel and shameful death. And in these words, "If I could suffer more, I would suffer more," I saw that as often as he could die, so often he would. Love would never let him have rest until he had done it. And I watched with great diligence to know how often he would die if he could. And truly the number passed my understanding and my wits so far that my reason could not comprehend it.

And when he had died so often, still he would count it as nothing for love. For he thinks everything is little compared to his love. Even though the sweet humanity of Christ could suffer only once, his goodness can never stop offering. Every day he is ready to do the same, if it could be. For if he said he would, for love of me, make new heavens and new earths, that was little in his sight. He could do this each day, if he wanted, without any effort. But to die for love of me so often that the number passes a creature's reason, this is the highest offer our Lord God might make to a human soul, as I see it.

Then he said this: "How should it be, then, that I should not do everything for your love that I could? It would not grieve me at all, since I would die so often for love of you, having no regard for my hard pains." And here I saw a second way of looking at his blessed passion. The love that made him suffer it surpasses his pains as far as heaven is above the earth. For the pain was a noble, precious, and honorable deed done in time by the working of love. And love was without beginning and will be without end. For this love he said this word with all sweetness: "If I could suffer more, I would suffer more." He did not say, "If it were needful to suffer more," but "If I could suffer more." For even if it were not needful, if he could suffer more, he would. This deed and work for our salvation was ordained as well as God could ordain it. It was done as honorably as Christ could do it. And in this I saw complete bliss in Christ, for his bliss would not have been complete if it could have been done any better than it was done.

And in these three words, "It is a joy, a bliss, an endless delight to me," were shown three heavens. For the joy, I understood the pleasing of the Father, and for the bliss the honor of the Son, and for the endless delight the Holy Spirit. The Father is pleased, the Son is honored, the Holy Spirit delights. And here I saw the third way of looking at his blessed passion, that is to say the joy and bliss that delights the Spirit. For our courteous Lord showed me his passion in five ways. The first is the bleeding of the head, the second is the discoloring of his blessed face, the third is the plentiful bleeding of his body from the scourging, the fourth is the deep drying, and the fifth is this about the joy and the bliss of the passion.

It is God's will that we have true delight with God in our salvation and that we be mightily comforted and strengthened. And so God wants our souls to be occupied joyfully with God's grace. For we are God's bliss, for God delights in us without end, and so, by God's grace, will we delight in God. All that he does for us and has done and ever will do was never costly to him nor could be, except only what he did in our humanity, beginning at the sweet incarnation and lasting to the blessed rising on Easter morning. Indeed, that is how long the cost of our redemption lasted, for which he always and endlessly rejoices, as was said before.

All of the Trinity worked in Christ's passion, ministering an abundance of virtues and plenteous grace to us through him. But only the virgin's son suffered to the rejoicing of all the blessed Trinity. This was shown in this word: "Are you well pleased?" By the other word Christ said, "If you are well pleased, I am well pleased," as if he had said, "It is joy and delight enough to me, and I ask nothing else of you for my effort but that I might please you."

And in this he brought to my mind the property of a glad giver. Always a glad giver pays little attention to the thing he gives, but all his desire and intent is to please and comfort the one to whom he gives. And if the receiver takes the gift gladly and thankfully, then the courteous giver counts all his cost and effort as nothing, because of the joy and delight he has and because he has pleased and comforted the one he loves.

All Will Be Well

From Chapters 27–28, Thirteenth Revelation

Julian deals briefly with the tenth, eleventh, and twelfth revelations, visions of Christ's heart split in two for the love of us, of the Virgin Mary at the cross, and of Christ glorified. She then spends thirty-seven chapters in extended reflection on the next two revelations, when all that she has seen comes together in an understanding of the depth of God's love for us in Christ.

After this, our Lord brought to my mind the longing that I had for him before. I saw that nothing held me back but sin, which I saw generally in all of us. I thought that if sin had never been, we would all have been clean and like our Lord as God made us. In my folly, before this time, I often wondered why, in the great foreseeing wisdom of God, the beginning of sin was not prevented. For then, I thought, all would have been well.

I should have abandoned this line of thought. Nevertheless, I mourned and worried about this without reason or discretion. But Jesus answered with this word: "Sin is necessary, but all will be well, and all will be well, and every kind of thing will be well." In this naked word, *sin*, our Lord brought to my mind in general all that is not good and the shameful hatred and uttermost tribulation that he bore for us in this life and his dying and all his pains and the suffering of all God's creatures, spiritually and bodily. For we are all troubled in part and will be troubled as we follow our master Jesus until our mortal flesh is completely purged of all our inward affections that are not very good.

Seeing this, with all the pains that ever were or ever will be, I understood the passion of Christ as the greatest pain, surpassing all. All this was shown in a touch and quickly changed over to comfort. For our good Lord does not want souls to be frightened by this ugly sight. But I did not see sin, for I believe it had no kind of substance or any part of being. It cannot be known except through the pain it causes. This pain is something, as I see it, for a while, because it purges us and makes us know ourselves and ask for mercy. The passion of our Lord is comfort to us against all this, and so is his blessed will. And for the tender love that our good Lord has for all who will be saved, he comforts quickly and sweetly, explaining in this way: "It is true that sin is the cause of all this pain, but all will be well, and every kind of thing will be well."

These words were shown quite tenderly, with no hint of blame toward me or to any who would be safe. So it was a great unkindness of me to blame or wonder about God for my sin, since God does not blame me for sin.

And in these same words I saw a high and marvelous secret hidden in God, which God will openly make known to us in heaven. In this knowledge we will truly see the reason why God allowed sin to come, which sight will give us endless joy.

So I saw how Christ has compassion on us because of sin. Just as I was earlier filled with pain and compassion from the passion of Christ, I was now in part filled with compassion for all my fellow Christians. For he really loves people who will be saved, that is to say, God's servants. The Holy Church will be shaken in sorrow and anguish and tribulation in this world as people shake a cloth in the wind. As to this, our Lord answered: "Ah, I shall make of this a great thing in heaven of endless honor and everlasting joy." Yes, to some degree I saw that our Lord rejoices in the tribulations of his servants with pity and compassion. In order to bring them into God's bliss, God lays on those God loves something that is no fault in God's sight but that will make them humbled and despised in this world, scorned and mocked and cast out. God does this to prevent the harm that the pomp and pride and vanity of this wretched life would give them, and make their way ready to come to heaven in everlasting bliss without end. For he says, "I do it all to break you of your vain affections and your vicious pride, and afterward I will gather you and make you meek and mild, clean and holy through unity with me."

And I saw that every kind of compassion that people have for their fellow Christians with love is Christ in them, and every self-denial that Christ showed in his passion is shown again in this compassion. This led to two ways of understanding our Lord's meaning. The one is the bliss that we are brought to, that he wants us to enjoy. The other is for comfort in our pain, for he wants us to know that it will all be turned to our honor and profit by virtue of his passion and that we never suffer all alone, but with him, and that we see him as our foundation. We see that his pains and tribulation so far pass all that we may suffer that it cannot be fully understood. Seeing this saves us from despair and begrudging our pains. Even if we see that our sin truly deserves pain, still his love excuses us. Of his great courtesy, he does away with all our blame and regards us with mercy and pity like innocent children.

Lives Turned from Sin

From Chapters 37–38, Thirteenth Revelation

As Julian continues to meditate on God's forgiveness of our sin, she offers examples of how God meets our sin and shame with divine love and blessing. John of Beverley was bishop of York and then retired to establish a monastery at Beverley where he died in 721. Julian knows him by reputation and perhaps by a visit to his shrine.

God brought to mind that I would sin, and for the delight that I had in beholding Christ, I did not listen readily to that revelation. Our Lord waited mercifully and gave me grace to listen. I took this revelation for myself alone. But by all the gracious comfort that follows, as you will see, I was taught to take it for all my fellow Christians—in general but not in particular.

Though our Lord showed me that I would sin, this should be understood to mean everyone. At this I felt a gentle fear, but our Lord answered, "I protect you most securely." This word was said with more love and assurance of spiritual protection than I can or may tell. For as it was shown earlier that I would sin, just so was the comfort shown: the assurance of protection for all my fellow Christians. What can make me love my fellow Christians more than to see that God loves all who will be saved as if they were all one soul? For in every soul that will be saved there is a godly will that never agrees to sin and never will. Just as there is a beastly will in the lower part that can will no good, just so is there a godly will in the higher part. That will is so good that it can never will evil, but always good. And so we are those whom God loves, and endlessly we do what delights God. Our good Lord showed this in the fullness of love that we stand in, in God's sight. Yes, God loves us as well now, while we are here, as God will when we are there before God's blessed face. It is the failure of love on our part that causes all our travail.

And God showed that sin will be no shame but bring honor to people. For just as truth answers every sin with pain, just so for every sin the same soul is given a blessing by love. Just as various sins are later punished with various pains to cause us grief, just so they will be rewarded with various joys in heaven for their victories, after they have been painful and sorrowful on earth. For the soul that will come to heaven is so precious to God and the place so full of honor that God's goodness never allows sin the last word with souls who will come there. But what kind of sinners shall be so rewarded is made known in Holy Church on earth and also in heaven by surpassing honors. For in this vision my understanding was lifted up to heaven. Then God simply brought to my mind David and others with him without number in the old law. And in the new law, God brought to my mind first Magdalene, Peter and Paul, Thomas of India, Saint John of Beverley, and others also without number. They are known in the church on earth with their sins, and it is no shame to them, but all is turned to their honor. And therefore our Lord shows for them here in part what is there shown in fullness. For there the token of sin is turned to honor.

And our Lord showed Saint John of Beverley most exalted to comfort us with a familiar example, and brought to my mind how he is a kind neighbor whom we know. And God called him Saint John of Beverley, as plainly as we do, and that with gladness and sweet cheer, showing that he is a most high saint in God's sight and fully blessed. God mentioned that in his youth and tender age he was a beloved servant of God, greatly loving and fearing God. And nevertheless God allowed him to fall, but protecting him mercifully so that he neither perished nor lost any time. Afterward God raised him to much more grace. By the contrition and meekness that he had during his life, God has given him many joys, surpassing what he would have had if he had never sinned or fallen. And God shows on earth that this is true, by performing many miracles near his body. All this was to make us glad and merry in love.

Hating Sin and Loving Sinners

From Chapters 39–40

Julian continues to reflect on God's love for sinners and hatred for sin.

Our good Lord protects us most preciously when it seems to us that we are nearly forsaken and cast away for our sin because we see that we have deserved it. Because of the meekness we gain from this, we are raised most high in God's sight by grace. Our Lord visits those he wants to with a special grace that causes great contrition and also compassion and a true desire for God to deliver them quickly from sin and pain. They are taken up to bliss and made equal to the saints. We are made clean by contrition, ready by compassion, and worthy by our true desire for God. These are three means, as I understood, by which all souls come to heaven, that is to say, those who have been sinners on earth and will be saved.

For it is necessary for every sinful soul to be healed by these medicines. Though they are healed, their wounds are still seen before God, not as wounds but as honors. On the other hand, as we are punished here with sorrow and penance, we will be rewarded in heaven by the courteous love of our God almighty, who wants none who come there to lose the reward of their efforts. For God regards sin as sorrow and pain to God's lovers, to whom, for love's sake, God assigns no blame.

The reward we seek will not be little, but high, glorious, and honorable. So all shame will turn to honor and joy. For our courteous Lord does not want his servants to despair over falling often or falling deeply. Our falling does not prevent him from loving us. Peace and love are always working in us, but we are not always in peace and love. God wants us to take heed that God is the foundation of all our whole life in love. Furthermore, God is our everlasting protector and mightily defends us against all our most dangerous and fierce enemies.

This is the sovereign friendship of our courteous Lord, who protects us so tenderly while we are in our sin. Furthermore, he touches us most secretly and shows us our sin by the sweet light of mercy and grace. But when we see ourselves so foul, then we expect God to be angry with us on account of our sin. And so we are stirred by the Holy Spirit to contrition and prayer and want with all our might to amend ourselves in order to soothe God's anger, until we find rest in our souls and our consciences are easy. Then we hope that God has forgiven our sin, which is the truth. Our courteous Lord shows himself to the soul simply and full of glad cheer, as if the soul had been in pain and in prison, saying, "My dear darling, I am glad you have come to me in all your sorrow. I have always been with you. Now you see me loving you, and we are united in bliss."

So sins are forgiven by grace and mercy, and the soul is honorably received in joy, just as it will be when it comes to heaven. This often happens by the gracious working of the Holy Spirit and the virtue of Christ's passion.

Here I understood truly that every kind of thing is made available to us by the great goodness of God, to such a degree that whenever we are ourselves in peace and love, we are truly safe. But since we may not have this in fullness while we are here, we need to live always in sweet prayer and lovely longing with our Lord Jesus. For he always longs to bring us to the fullness of joy. But now, because of all that has been said, if any man or woman is stirred by folly to say or think, *If this is true, then it is good to sin to have more reward*, or else to pay less attention to sin, beware! For truly, if it comes, it is untrue and of the enemy.

For the same true love that touches us all with blessed comfort, that same blessed love teaches us that we should hate only sin for love's sake. And I am sure through my own experience that the more kind souls see this in the courteous love of our Lord God, the more reluctant they are to sin and the more ashamed they are. For if all the pain that is in hell and in purgatory and on earth, death and all the rest, were laid before us, we would rather choose all that pain rather than sin. All is good except sin, and nothing evil but sin. When we set our will to love and meekness by the working of mercy and grace, we are made completely beautiful and clean.

Christ himself is the ground of all the laws of Christians, and he taught us to do good against evil. He is himself this love, and does to us as he teaches us to do. For he wants us to be like him in the wholeness of endless love to ourselves and our fellow Christians. God does not want our love for ourselves or our fellow Christians to be broken any more than God's own love for us is broken because of our sin. Instead, hate sin openly and endlessly love the soul as God loves it. For these words that God said are an endless comfort: "I protect you most securely."

Prayer

From Chapters 43–44, Fourteenth Revelation

In the fourteenth revelation, God teaches Julian about asking God's help through proper prayer and secure trust.

Prayer unites the soul to God. Though the soul is always like God by nature and in substance as restored by grace, it is often unlike God in condition through sin on our part. Then prayer is a witness that the soul wills as God wills, and it comforts the conscience and prepares us for grace. So God teaches us to pray for grace and trust mightily that we will receive it. For God regards us with love and wants to make us sharers of God's good will and deeds. Therefore God stirs us to pray that we may do what delights God. For this prayer and good will (that we have as God's gift), God will reward us endlessly. This was shown in this word: "If you ask it."

In this word God showed such great pleasure and delight as if God were greatly in our debt for each good deed that we do. Yet it is God who does them. We ask God mightily to do the very thing that delights him, as if the Sovereign said, "How could you please me more than to ask mightily, wisely, and willingly to do what I want done?" And so the soul is attuned to God by prayer.

But when our courteous Lord, as a special grace, shows himself to our souls, we have what we desire. Then for a time we cannot see what more we should ask. All our intention and strength is set wholly on beholding him. This is a high, imperceptible prayer, as I see it. The whole reason we pray is to be united in our vision with the one to whom we pray, marvelously rejoicing with reverent fear and such great sweetness and delight in God that for a while we can pray for nothing at all except as God moves us.

I know well that the more the soul sees of God, the more it desires God by grace. But when we do not see God in this way, then we feel the need to pray to Jesus for our failings and disabilities. For when a soul is tempted, troubled, and left to itself in unrest, then it is time to pray to become flexible and compliant for God. By no kind of prayer can we make God flexible toward us. For God is always the same in love. So I saw that whenever we see the need to pray, our Lord God follows us, helping our desire. And when we, through God's special grace, behold God plainly, seeing no other, then we have to follow God, and God draws us in by love. For I saw and felt that God's marvelous and overflowing goodness fills all our strength. Then I saw that God's continual working in every kind of thing is done so divinely, so wisely, and so mightily that it surpasses all our imagining and all that we can think or expect. Then we can do no more than behold God and rejoice with a high and mighty desire to be completely united with God and listen to God's urgings and rejoice in God's loving and delight in God's goodness.

So we will, with God's sweet grace, come into God now in this life through our own meek, continual prayer and by many secret touches of sweet spiritual visions and feelings, measured out by how much our simplicity can bear. This is done and will be done by the grace of the Holy Spirit until at last we die in longing for love. Then we will all come to our Lord, knowing ourselves clearly and having God abundantly. We will be endlessly hidden in God, truly seeing and abundantly feeling and spiritually hearing and delectably smelling and sweetly tasting God. There we will see God face-to-face, simply and fully. The creature who was made will see and endlessly behold God, who is the Maker. For no one can see God and live afterward, that is to say, in this mortal life. But when, as a special grace, God wants to reveal himself here, God strengthens the creature above itself and measures the revelation according to God's own will. That is profitable for the time being.

Truth sees God, and wisdom beholds God, and from these two comes the third, and that is a marvelous delight in God, which is love. Where truth and wisdom are, truly there is love, coming from both of them. All are of God's making. For God is endless sovereign truth, endless sovereign wisdom, endless sovereign uncreated love. The human soul is a creature in which God has created the same properties. More and more it does what it was made for: it sees God and beholds God and loves God. So God rejoices in the creature and the creature in God, endlessly marveling. In this marveling we see our God, our Lord, our Maker, so high, great, and good in comparison to us creatures that we scarcely seem anything at all to ourselves. But the brightness and clearness of truth and wisdom make us see and know that we are made for love. And in this love God protects us forever.

●

Mercy and Grace

From Chapters 47–48, Fourteenth Revelation

Julian returns to the theme of God's mercy and grace, comparing and contrasting the two as different aspects of God's love.

There are two things that our souls owe as debts. One is that we reverently marvel. The other is that we meekly suffer, always rejoicing in God. For God wants us to know that we will shortly see clearly in God all that we desire. Notwithstanding all this, I saw and marveled greatly at the mercy and forgiveness of God. I understood from earlier teaching that the mercy of God is the forgiveness of God's anger after we have sinned. I thought that to a soul whose expectation and desire is to love, the anger of God would be worse than any other pain. So I understood that the forgiveness of God's anger should be one of the principal points of God's mercy. But no matter how I looked and wished, I could not see this point in any of the revelations.

This is how I understood the working of mercy. People are changeable in this life and, through simplicity and lack of cunning, fall into sin. They are unmighty and unwise by themselves, and their wills are overwhelmed when they are storm-tossed and in sorrow and woe. The reason is blindness: they do not see God. For if they saw God continually, they would have no mischievous feelings or any other kind of stirring or the sorrowing that leads to sin.

So I saw and felt at the same time, and I thought that the sight and feeling were high and plenteous and gracious as regards our common feeling in this life. Yet I thought it was low and small as regards the great desire souls have to see God. I felt in myself five kinds of activity: rejoicing, mourning, desire, fear, and true hope. Rejoicing because God gave me knowledge and understanding that it was truly God that I saw; mourning, and that was for failing; desire that I might see God ever more and more, understanding and knowing that we will never have complete rest until we see God clearly and truly in heaven; fear was because it seemed to me the whole time that sight would fail and I would be left by myself; true hope was in the endless love, for I saw that I would be protected by God's mercy and brought to bliss.

Rejoicing in God's sight with true hope of God's merciful protection gave me a feeling of comfort, so that the mourning and fear were not greatly painful. Yet in all this I saw through God's revelation that this kind of vision of God may not be constant in this life, for the sake of God's honor and the increase of our endless joy. So our vision of God often fails and we fall into ourselves. Then we find ourselves feeling nothing but the contradictions in ourselves and all that follows the old root of our first sin through continuing to sin ourselves. In this we are beaten down and tempted with feeling of sin and of pain in many different ways, spiritual and bodily, as they are known to us in this life.

But our good Lord, the Holy Spirit, who is endless life dwelling in our souls, truly protects us and works in us a peace and puts us at ease by grace and makes us compliant and attuned to God. This is the mercy and the way that our good Lord continually leads us in, as long as we are in this changeable life. For I saw no anger except on our part, and God forgives that in us, for anger is nothing but a perversity and contrariness to peace and love. It comes from lack of strength or lack of wisdom or lack of goodness. This lack is not in God, but on our part. For we, by sin and wretchedness, have in us an anger and continual contrariness to peace and love. God showed that often enough in the lovely cheer of mercy and pity. For the ground of mercy is in love, and the action of mercy is our protection in love.

That is to say, as I see it, mercy is a sweet, gracious action in love, mingled with plentiful pity. For mercy works to protect us and to turn everything to our good. For love's sake, mercy allows us to fail in some measure. As much as we fail, so much we fall. As much as we fall, so much we die. It is right for us to die in as much as we lack a vision and a feeling of God who is our life. Our failing is fearful, our falling is shameful, and our dying is sorrowful.

Yet in all this the sweet eye of pity and love never leaves us, and the work of mercy never stops. For I saw the property of mercy and the property of grace, which have two ways of working in one love. Mercy is a pity-filled property, which belongs to motherhood in tender love. Grace is an honorable property, which belongs to royal lordship in the same love. Mercy works by protecting, permitting, reviving, and healing, all through the tenderness of love. Grace works with mercy, raising, rewarding, endlessly surpassing what our loving and effort deserve, spreading abroad and showing the high, plentiful largesse of God's royal lordship in God's marvelous courtesy. This is from the abundance of love, for grace works our fearful failing into plentiful and endless solace. And grace works our shameful falling into high, honorable rising. And grace works our sorrowful dying into holy, blissful life.

For I most truly saw that as our contrariness always works on earth to bring us pain, shame, and sorrow, just so grace on the contrary works in heaven to bring us solace, honor, and bliss, surpassing to such a degree that when we come up and receive the sweet reward that grace has made for us, there we will thank and bless our Lord, endlessly rejoicing that we ever suffered sorrow.

The Motherhood of God

Julian returns to the contrast between mercy as motherly love and grace as lordly love. Here she pushes the idea even farther to talk about the motherhood of God revealed in Christ, who not only brings us to new birth through grace, but brought all creation to birth, as John says, "All things came into being through him, and without him not one thing came into being" (John 1:3, NRSV).

As truly as God is our Father, so truly is God our Mother. God showed that in everything, especially in these sweet words that God says: "It is I." That is to say, "It is I, the might and goodness of fatherhood. It is I, the wisdom and kindness of motherhood. It is I, the light and the grace that is all blessed love. It is I, the Trinity. It is I, the Unity. It is I, the high, sovereign goodness of every kind of thing. It is I who makes you love. It is I who makes you long. It is I, the endless fulfillment of all true desires." For there the soul is most high, noble, and honorable and also most lowly, meek, and mild.

From this substantial ground we have all our virtues of the sensual life as natural gifts, and through the help of mercy and grace, without which we can gain nothing. Our high Father, almighty God, who is Being, knew us and loved us from before time began. Because of this knowing and the eternal foreseeing advice of the blessed Trinity, God, in marvelous deep love, wanted the second person to become our Mother, our Brother, and our Savior. So it follows that as truly as God is our Father, so truly is God our Mother. Our Father wills, our Mother works, our good Lord the Holy Spirit confirms. And so it belongs to us to love our God in whom we have our being, reverently thanking and praising God for making us, mightily praying to our Mother for mercy and pity and to our Lord the Holy Spirit for help and grace. For in these three is all our life, nature, mercy, and grace. From these come mildness, patience, and pity and hating of sin and wickedness. For it is distinctive of the virtues to hate sin and wickedness.

So Jesus is our true Mother by nature through our first creation, and he is our true Mother by grace through taking on our created nature. All the fair working and sweet, kindly office of beloved motherhood is appropriate to the second person, for in Christ we have this goodly will, whole and safe without end, both in nature and in grace, of his own distinctive goodness.

I understood three ways of looking at the motherhood of God. The first is the ground of creating our nature. The second is taking on our nature, the beginning of the motherhood of grace. The third is the motherhood of working, through which grace spreads forth in length and breadth, height and depth without end. And all is one love.

Our natural Mother, our gracious Mother, since he wished to become completely our Mother in every way, took the foundation of his work in a lowly and mild manner in the maiden's womb. That is to say our high God, the sovereign wisdom of all, bedecked himself willingly in our poor flesh in this low place so that he himself could perform the service and office of motherhood for all things. A mother's service is nearest, quickest, and surest: nearest because it is most natural, quickest because it is most loving, and surest because it is truest. No one could ever perform this office to the fullest except Christ alone. We know that all our mothers bear us into a world of pain and death. Ah, what is that? But our true Mother Jesus alone bears us into a world of joy and endless life, may he be blessed. So he carried us with him in love and distress, until the time when he would suffer the sharpest thorns and most grievous pains that ever were or ever will be and died at last. And when he had done that and so carried us to bliss, even this could not complete his marvelous love. He showed that in these high, surpassing words of love: "If I could suffer more, I would suffer more." He could not die again, but he would not stop working.

So it is only right that he should nourish us, since his precious motherly love makes him feel he owes us. A mother may give her child her milk to suck, but our precious Mother Jesus feeds us with himself. He does this most courteously and tenderly with the blessed sacrament, the precious food of true life. With all the sweet sacraments he sustains us most mercifully and graciously, which is what he meant by these blessed words: "It is I whom Holy Church preaches and teaches to you." That is to say, "All the health and the life of the sacraments, all the virtue and grace of my words, all the goodness that is ordained in the Holy Church for you, it is I."

A mother may lay her child tenderly to her breast, but our tender Mother Jesus may simply lead us into his blessed breast by his sweet open side and show us there, in part, the Godhead and the joys of heaven with spiritual assurance of endless bliss. He showed that in the tenth revelation, giving the same understanding in this sweet word, "See how I love you," looking into his blessed side and rejoicing.

This fair, lovely word, *Mother*, is so sweet and kind in itself that it may not be truly said of any or to any but of and to him who is the true Mother of life and everything. The properties of motherhood are nature, love, wisdom, and knowledge, and it is God. A kind, loving mother who knows the needs of her child protects it most tenderly, according to the nature and condition of motherhood. And as it grows in age and stature, she changes what she does for it but not her love. When it has grown even older, she allows it to be punished in order to break down its vices and to make the child receive virtues and graces.

Our Lord does this and all that is fair and good in those by whom it is done. So he is our Mother in nature through the working of grace in lower matters for love of the higher. He wants us to know it, for he wants to have all our love fastened on him. In this I saw that every debt we owe to fatherhood and motherhood according to God's commandment is fulfilled in truly loving God, which blessed love Christ brings about in us. This was shown in everything, especially in the high, plentiful words, "It is I whom you love."

Motherly Discipline and Love

From Chapter 61, Fourteenth Revelation

Julian continues to compare God's love to the tender care of a mother who will even allow her children to make mistakes so that they may learn by them.

In bringing us forth spiritually, Christ shows more tenderness in protecting us beyond any comparison, since the soul is of more value in his sight. He kindles our understanding, he prepares our ways, he eases our consciences, he comforts our souls, he lightens our hearts, and he gives us partial knowing and loving of his blessed Godhead with gracious remembrance of his sweet humanity and his blessed passion and with courteous marveling at his high, surpassing goodness. He causes us to love all that he loves for the sake of his love and to be well pleased with him and all his works. When we fall, he quickly raises us by his loving call and gracious touch. When we are strengthened by his sweet working, then we willingly choose, by his grace, to serve and love him everlastingly without end.

Yet after this he allows some of us to fall more severely and grievously than we ever did before, so we think. Then we, who are not all-wise, think that everything we had begun is nothing. But that is not so, for we needed to fall and to see it. If we never fell, we would not know how feeble and wretched we are by ourselves nor would we know so fully the marvelous love of our Maker.

We will see truly in heaven without end that we have grievously sinned in this life. Notwithstanding this, we shall see that we were never hurt in his love nor ever less precious in his sight. So by the experience of this falling, we will have a high and marvelous knowledge of God's love without end. Strong and marvelous is the love that cannot and will not be broken because of trespass.

This is one understanding of what we gain, and the other is the lowliness and meekness that we will get by seeing our falling. Through this we will be highly raised in heaven, which might never have happened without that meekness. So we had to see it, and if we do not see it, falling would not be any gain for us. Commonly we fall first and then we see it. Both come from God's mercy.

A mother may allow a child to fall sometimes and be distressed in various ways for its own benefit, but out of love can never allow any kind of danger to come to her child. And though our earthly mother may allow her child to perish, our heavenly Mother Jesus can never allow us who are his children to perish. For he is almighty and all wisdom and all love and none is like him, may he be blessed.

Often when our falling and our wretchedness are shown to us, we are so fearful and greatly ashamed of ourselves that we scarcely know where to hide. But then our courteous Mother does not want us to flee away. Nothing would suit him less. He wants us then to act like little children. For when they are distressed and afraid, they run quickly to their mother. If they can do no more, they cry to their mother for help with all their might. That is what he wants us to do, like a meek child, saying, "My kind Mother, my gracious Mother, my beloved Mother, have mercy on me. I have made myself foul and displeasing to you, and I cannot change it except with your help and grace."

And if we do not feel better then, we can be sure that he is acting like a wise mother. For if he sees that it is profitable for us to mourn and weep, he allows it with mercy and pity until the best time to show love. He wants us to behave like children who more and more naturally love their mother in well-being and in woe. And he wants us to take hold mightily on the faith of Holy Church and find there our beloved Mother in comfort and true understanding together with all the blessed community. For one single person may often be broken, but the whole body of Holy Church was never broken nor ever will be without end. And so it is a sure thing and a good and gracious one to want meekly and mightily to be fastened and united to our Mother Holy Church, which is Christ Jesus. For the flood of mercy that is his beloved blood and precious water is plentiful enough to make us fair and clean. The blessed wounds of our Savior are open and rejoice to heal us. The sweet, gracious hands of our Mother are ready and diligent around us. For in all this working he fills the office of a kind nurse who has nothing else to do but pay attention to the salvation of her child.

It is his office to save us, his honor to do it, and his will that we know it. He wants us to love him sweetly and trust in him meekly and mightily. And he showed this in these gracious words, "I protect you most securely."

Impatience and Fear

From Chapters 73–74, Sixteenth Revelation

After a fifteenth revelation, a promise of heaven, the revelations ceased. The first began about four in the morning and the last ended about three in the afternoon. As Julian began to recover, she doubted her visions as the ravings of a fevered mind. The next night, she dreamed of demons attacking her and then of Christ enthroned in the heavenly city. He said to her, "Understand it well, it was no raving you saw today. Take it and believe it and hold fast to it and comfort yourself with it and trust in it, and you will not be overcome." This was her final revelation.

Our Lord God showed all this blessed teaching in three ways: by bodily sight and by words formed in my understanding and by spiritual sight. For the bodily sight, I have said what I saw as truly as I can. For the words, I have told them just as our Lord showed them to me. For the spiritual sight, I have said some, but I can never tell it fully. So I am moved to say more about this spiritual sight, as God will give me grace.

God showed two kinds of sickness that we have. One is impatience or sloth, for we bear our pain and suffering heavily.

The other is despair or doubtful fear, as I will explain later. God showed sin in general, which includes everything, but in particular none but these two. These are the two that most vex and trouble us, as our Lord showed me, of which God wants us to be cured. I speak of such men and women who for God's love hate sin and are disposed to do God's will. Then by our spiritual blindness and bodily heaviness we are most inclined to these sins. Therefore it is God's will that they be known. Then we would refuse them as we do other sins.

For help against this, our Lord most meekly showed the patience that he had in his hard passion and also the joy and delight he has from that passion because of his love. He showed this as a model that we should gladly and easily bear our pains, for that is greatly pleasing to him and endlessly profitable to us. The reason we are bothered by them is because of ignorance of love. We are most blind about this subject, for some of us believe that God is almighty and may do all, that God is all-wise and can do all. But that God is all love and will do all, there we fail. It is this ignorance that most hinders those who love God, as I see it. When we begin to hate sin and amend ourselves by the ordinances of Holy Church, there remains a fear that holds us back from looking at ourselves and the sins of the past or even our everyday sins. We do not keep our promise or maintain the cleanness that our Lord gives us but often fall into so much wretchedness that it is a shame to say it. Looking at this makes us so sorry and heavy that we can scarcely see any comfort. Sometimes we take this fear as meekness, but it is a foul blindness and weakness. We cannot despise it as we do another sin that we recognize as coming from lack of true judgment and being against truth. For of all the properties of the blessed Trinity, it is God's will that we have the most faithfulness and delight in love.

For love makes might and wisdom most meek to us. Just as God is courteous to forgive us our sin after we repent, so God wants us to forget our sin in regard to our unskillful heaviness and our doubtful fear.

For I understood four kinds of fear. One is fright. It comes to us suddenly through frailty. This fear does good, for it helps to purge us as does bodily sickness or other kinds of pain that are not sin. All such pains help us if they are accepted patiently. The second is fear of pain, by which we are stirred and wakened from the sleep of sin. Those who are fast asleep in sin are not able for the time being to receive the soft comfort of the Holy Spirit until they have experienced this fear of pain from bodily death and spiritual enemies. This fear stirs us to seek comfort and mercy from God. So this fear helps us as an entrance and enables us to have contrition through the blessed touching of the Holy Spirit. The third is doubtful fear. Since doubtful fear draws us to despair, God wants to have it turned into love through true knowledge of love. That is to say, the bitterness of doubt is turned into the sweetness of kind love by grace, for it never pleases our Lord that God's servants doubt divine goodness. The fourth is reverent fear. There is no fear that fully pleases God in us but reverent fear. It is soft, because the more we have it, the less we feel it because of the sweetness of love.

Love and fear are siblings, rooted in us by the goodness of our Maker. They will never be taken from us forever. We have to love through our nature, and we have to love through grace. We have to fear through our nature, and we have to fear through grace. Reverent fear pertains to the lordship and fatherhood of God as love pertains to the goodness. And though this reverent fear and love are not both the same, yet neither may be had without the other.

Therefore I am sure that whoever loves also fears, though it is felt but little. That fear makes us flee from all that is not good and fall into our Lord's breast, like a child in the mother's arms, knowing our feebleness and great need, knowing God's everlasting goodness and blessed love, only seeking salvation in God, clinging with faithful trust. The fear that brings us to such action is natural and gracious and good and true. Thus we will be simple through love and near to God, and through fear be gentle and courteous to God.

So we ask of our Lord God that we may fear God reverently and love God meekly and trust in God mightily. For when we fear God reverently and love God meekly, our trust is never in vain. The more we trust and the more mightily we trust, the more we please and honor our Lord in whom we trust. And if we lack this reverent fear and meek love, as God forbid we should, our trust will soon go astray for a while. So we need greatly to pray to our Lord for grace that we may have the gift of this reverent fear and meek love in heart and work. For without this no one can please God.

Penance

From Chapters 81–82, Sixteenth Revelation

In this passage Julian continues to review and expand on the spiritual visions that, she realizes, can never be fully explained.

It is the greatest honor to God of all that we can do that we live gladly and simply for God's love in our penance. For God regards us so tenderly as to see all our living here to be penance. For our natural longing for God is a lasting penance in us, which God brings about in us and mercifully helps us to bear. God's love makes God long for us, but God's wisdom and truth with divine justice make God allow us to stay here, so God sees this as penance for us. This is our natural penance and the highest, as I see it. For this penance never leaves us until we are fulfilled and will have God as our reward.

Therefore God wants us to set our hearts on passing over from the pain that we feel to the bliss that we trust.

But here our courteous Lord showed the moaning and mourning of the soul, explaining, "I know well that you want to live for my love, simply and gladly bearing all the penance that may come to you. But since you do not live without sin, therefore you are heavy and sorrowful. Even if you could live without sin, you would bear all the woe that might come to you for my love, and that is the truth. Do not be overly grieved with sin that happens to you against your will."

Here I understood that the Lord beheld the servant with pity and not with blame. For in this passing life we cannot expect to live completely without sin. God loves us endlessly, and we sin out of habit and God shows it to us most mildly. Then we sorrow and mourn discreetly, turning to behold God's mercy, clinging to God's love and goodness, seeing that God is our medicine, knowing that all we do is sin.

Thus, through the meekness we gain from seeing our sin, faithfully knowing God's everlasting love and thanking and praising God, we please God. "I love you and you love me and our love will never be broken in two. For your gain I suffer." All this was shown in spiritual understanding along with this blessed word, "I protect you most securely."

By the great desire that I saw in our blessed Lord that we should live in this manner, that is to say in longing and rejoicing as all this lesson of love shows, I understood that everything that is contrary to this is not of God, but of the enemy. God wants us to know this by the sweet, gracious light of God's kind love.

In falling and in rising we are always kept preciously in one love. For in beholding God we do not fall, and in beholding ourselves we do not stand. Both of these are true, as I see it, but beholding our Lord God is the higher truth. Then we are bound to God, which is what God wants in showing us this higher truth. I understood that while we are in this life, it is very beneficial to us that we see these both at once. For the higher beholding keeps us in spiritual joy and true rejoicing in God while the other, the lower beholding, keeps us in fear and makes us ashamed of ourselves.

Our good Lord always wants us to hold fast to beholding the higher and not leave off knowledge of the lower until we are brought up above where we will have our Lord Jesus as our reward and be filled full of joy and bliss without end.

The Last Word: Love

From Chapter 86, Epilogue

This book was begun by God's gift and grace, but I have not yet lived it out completely, as I see it. For love's sake, let us all pray that we may work together with God, thanking, trusting, rejoicing. That is the prayer our good Lord wants, as I understand what I gained of God's meaning and in the sweet words that God says most simply, "I am the foundation of your asking." Truly I saw and understood our Lord's meaning that God showed all this because the Maker wants it known more than it is. In this knowledge God will give us grace to love God and cling to God. For God's own heavenly treasure (so greatly loved on earth that God will give us more light) and solace in heavenly joy is in drawing our hearts from the sorrow and darkness we are in.

From the time that it was revealed, I often desired to know what our Lord's meaning was. After more than fifteen years, I was answered in spiritual understanding, "What? Would you know your Lord's meaning in this thing? Know it well: love was the meaning. Who showed it to you? Love. What did God show you? Love. Why did God show it? For love. Hold on to that, and you will understand more of the same. But apart from that, you will never understand anything.

So I was taught that love is our Lord's meaning. I saw most surely in this and in all that our God made that God loved us, and this love never was satisfied and never will be. All God's works have been done in this love, and in this love God has made everything that is for our benefit, and in this love our life is everlasting. In our creation, we had a beginning, but the love in which God made us was in God without beginning. In this love we have our beginning. All this we will see in God without end.

Appendix

Reading Spiritual Classics for Personal and Group Formation

Many Christians today are searching for more spiritual depth, for something more than simply being good church members. That quest may send them to the spiritual practices of New Age movements or of Eastern religions such as Zen Buddhism. Christians, though, have their own long spiritual tradition, a tradition rich with wisdom, variety, and depth.

The great spiritual classics testify to that depth. They do not concern themselves with mystical flights for a spiritual elite. Rather, they contain very practical advice and insights that can support and shape the spiritual growth of any Christian. We can all benefit by sitting at the feet of the masters (both male and female) of Christian spirituality.

Reading spiritual classics is different from most of the reading we do. We have learned to read to master a text and extract information from it. We tend to read quickly, to get through a text. And we summarize as we read, seeking the main point. In reading spiritual classics, though, we allow the text to master and form us. Such formative reading goes more slowly, more reflectively, allowing time for God to speak to us through the text. God's word for us may come as easily from a minor point or even an aside as from the major point.

Formative reading requires that you approach the text in humility. Read as a seeker, not an expert. Don't demand that the text meet your expectations for what an "enlightened" author should write. Humility means accepting the author as another imperfect human, a product of his or her own time and situation. Learn to celebrate what is foundational in an author's writing without being overly disturbed by what is peculiar to the author's life and times. Trust the text as a gift from both God and the author, offered to you for your benefit— to help you grow in Christ.

To read formatively, you must also slow down. Feel free to reread a passage that seems to speak specially to you. Stop from time to time to reflect on what you have been reading. Keep a journal for these reflections. Often the act of writing can itself prompt further, deeper reflection. Keep your notebook open and your pencil in hand as you read. You might not get back to that wonderful insight later. Don't worry that you are not getting through an entire passage—or even the first paragraph! Formative reading is about depth rather than breadth, quality rather than quantity. As you read, seek God's direction for your own life. Timeless truths have their place but may not be what is most important for your own formation here and now.

As you read the passage, you might keep some of these questions running through your mind:

- How is what I'm reading true of my own life? Where does it reflect my own *experience*?
- How does this text challenge me? What new *direction* does it offer me?
- What must I change to put what I am reading into practice? How can I *incarnate* it, let this word become flesh in my life?

You might also devote special attention to sections that upset you. What is the source of the disturbance? Do you want to argue theology? Are you turned off by cultural differences? Or have you been skewered by an insight that would turn your life upside down if you took it seriously? Let your journal be a dialogue with the text.

If you find yourself moving from reading the text to chewing over its implications to praying, that's great! Spiritual reading is really the first step in an ancient way of prayer called *lectio divina* or "divine reading." Reading leads naturally into reflection on what you have read (meditation). As you reflect on what the text might mean for your life, you may well want to ask for God's help in living out any new insights or direction you have perceived (prayer). Sometimes such prayer may lead you further into silently abiding in God's presence (contemplation). And, of course, the process is only really completed when it begins to make a difference in the way we live (incarnation).

As good as it is to read spiritual classics in solitude, it is even better to join with others in a small group for mutual formation or "spiritual direction in common." This is *not* the same as a study group that talks about spiritual classics. A group for mutual formation would have similar goals as for an individual's reading: to allow the text to shine its light on the *experiences* of the group members, to suggest new *directions* for their lives and practical ways of *incarnating* these directions. Such a group might agree to focus on one short passage from a classic at each meeting (even if members have read more). Discussion usually goes much deeper if all the members have already read and reflected on the passage before the meeting and bring their journals.

Such groups need to watch for several potential problems. It is easy to go off on a tangent (especially if it takes the focus off the members' own experience and onto generalities). At such times a group leader might bring the group's attention back to the text: "What does our author say about that?" Or, "How do we experience that in our own lives?" When a group member shares a problem, others may be tempted to try to "fix" it. This is much less helpful than sharing similar experiences and how they were handled (for good or ill). "Sharing" someone else's problems (whether that person is in or out of the group) should be strongly discouraged.

One person could be designated as leader, to be responsible for opening and closing prayers; to be the first to share or respond to the text; and to keep notes during the discussion to highlight recurring themes, challenges, directives, or practical steps. These responsibilities could also be shared among several members of the group or rotated.

For further information about formative reading of spiritual classics, try *A Practical Guide to Spiritual Reading* by Susan Annette Muto. *Shaped by the Word: The Power of Scripture in Spiritual Formation* by M. Robert Mulholland Jr. covers formative reading of the Bible. *Good Things Happen: Experiencing Community in Small Groups* by Dick Westley is an excellent resource on forming small groups of all kinds.

CPSIA information can be obtained
at www.ICGtesting.com
Printed in the USA
FFOW02n0429181217
44082628-43481FF